life's
toolbox
...blueprints
included

brian j plachta

Published in Grand Rapids, Michigan.

The author is grateful to Ralph M. Annunziata at nunziWorx.com for his cover design, interior layout and photography & Sandy Kingsland at Kingsland Ace Hardware for the 'tools' and the use of Kingsland Hardware, kingslandace@sbcglobal.net.

The term *Pillars of Steel* and its acronym, *POS* are used throughout the book in reference to the Men's Initiative of the same name. *Pillars of Steel* is a men's initiative guided by the *POS* definition of masculine spirituality:

The ongoing endeavor to develop and deepen our relationship with God and each other together as men in the company of others.

In a contemplative spirit, *POS* strives to:
- Listen
- Discern, and
- Collaborate with other individuals, groups and organizations to

help them create and sustain on-going opportunities for men to enrich their wisdom and understanding about life.

For further information about *Pillars of Steel* and its work visit: www.pillarsofsteel.org.

The *Life's Toolbox* book and its companion *Facilitator's Guide* may be purchased in bulk for educational, business, fund-raising, church programming or other adult education uses. For information, please email: brian@pillarsofsteel.org.

ISBN: 978-0-692-21856-3. Library of Congress: 2014908837.

Printed in the United States of America

Dedication

Life's Toolbox & its companion,
Facilitator's Guide are dedicated to the memory
of my father, Joe Plachta, who died when I was 16.
It may have taken me a couple of decades but,
I finally know deep in my heart Dad,
I've had your blessing all along.

toolbox

contents

life
making it my project

introduction

Like a lot of men I like to fix things. Give me a project and I'll tackle it. Give me a problem and I'll solve it.

But life? Sometimes I haven't got a clue.

For me it's a project that's hard to tackle much less solve.

I struggle with:
- Dealing with the stuff that ticks me off.
- Facing my fear.
- Handling the continual challenges life throws at me.

The Problem: An Empty Toolbox

Far too often I follow what I refer to as the man code. Pretending everything is fine—refusing to stop and ask for directions when needed.

That makes life's everyday struggles tougher because, as a typical man, I end up going it alone.

But when I fly solo, I overlook the tools other guys use and the wisdom they may offer in understanding and overcoming life's challenges. As a result, I stay locked in my own mental gyrations ignoring the new ideas and fresh perspectives I can gain from other men on the journey.

This leaves me trying to handle life with an

empty toolbox.

The Solution: Jam-packed Toolboxes

I believe it's time to change and for men to grab a seat at the workbench, sit down, and figure out what tools we really need in our toolboxes to become master craftsmen at this project called life. Once we discover the tools to handle life successfully, doors open and we can grow (a lot) from each other.

Where To Start

In this guide we're going to look at our fears along with other problems in a new way. Not as something to battle with or stuff under the rug. Instead as good things that help us grow wiser and stronger.

This guide invites us to a deeper wisdom about how fears are like caution signs. Once properly understood, our fears point us toward a new insight that is often hidden beneath what is bothering us.

Along the way we'll look at the lives of some heroes who've faced their struggles head-on and overcome them—men who inspire us to grow.

We'll also gain a fresh perspective on how to fix life's problems. We'll address our fears by talking about them, laying them out on the workbench, and naming the common challenges we face so we can figure out how to move through and beyond them.

An Invitation

Use this short guide to begin unrolling some of the blueprints necessary to understand life. Discover how the challenges faced by men are not obstacles, but rather opportunities in which to grow. Growth which provides us with :

- Wholeness.
- Balance.
- Peace.
- Happiness.

So, let's roll up our sleeves, and discover the tools we need to pack into our life toolboxes. Tools that provide us with new insight, deeper perspectives, and wisdom about ourselves, others, and our project: - LIFE.

POW'R GARD

PORTABLE GENERATOR

ID 2536101

Where do I find my power? Tap into the

generator

1

When the power goes out at our home or business, we can plug into a generator to get electricity. The generator keeps the lights, heat, and electrical appliances functioning. Those things we rely upon for basic survival. It's the same thing with our inner power.

God–our higher power–is like a generator. He's the source of our inner energy–a life-source that provides guidance, direction, and purpose. Wisdom.

Plugging into a power greater than ourselves connects us with the source of our being, like an inner flashlight. Unplugged from our generator our inner energy eventually runs out. When that happens, soon we're running on empty. We become lethargic. Lost. Numb.

The question of whether we believe God exists is one of life's most important questions. Our belief in a source of power greater than ourselves shapes our views of life, humanity, morality, and destiny.

There are many theories we can look toward to try and help us determine if God exists or not. Perhaps a tool many find most tangible is whether I *experience* God.

- When I stand barefoot at the edge of a pebbled beach with waves pounding against my feet, fully alive to the mystery of a tangerine sun dipping slowly into the water, a whoosh of air rushes up from within my gut flooding my body with a sense of awe. In that moment, beyond mere words, I sense a connection with a vast power watching over and delighting in me, and in all of creation.

- When I'm struggling with a problem and a sudden blast of insight wells up from within, I know I have connected with a deeper wisdom beyond myself.
- When I'm filled with despair, and an unexpected person steps into my life restoring my hope, I trust God has reached out to touch me.

In those moments of felt-experience, we sense the presence of a life force larger than ourselves that holds us, contains us, fuels us, and is guiding us home. When we experience those moments, the divine becomes real. God-in-flesh.

Heroes.

Author Stephen King, says he chooses to believe in God because of his personal experiences of a divine being.

"If you don't believe in God then you're missing the stars in the sky and you're missing the sunrises and sunsets and you're missing the fact that bees pollinate all these crops and keep us alive and the way that everything seems to work together. Everything is sort of built in a way that to me suggests intelligent design."

Though King struggles with the institutional

church due to its human element, which has often skewed our true understanding of God, he believes we cannot dismiss the existence of a God who loves, cares and creates in, and through us.

Asking ourselves the fundamental question about whether we believe in God or not and coming to a deeper experience of that truth, is a critical part of keeping ourselves connected with the source of our power–our generator.

Deeper Wisdom.
I believe in [God]
as I believe that the sun has risen;
not only because I see it,
but because by it I see everything else.
- C. S. Lewis

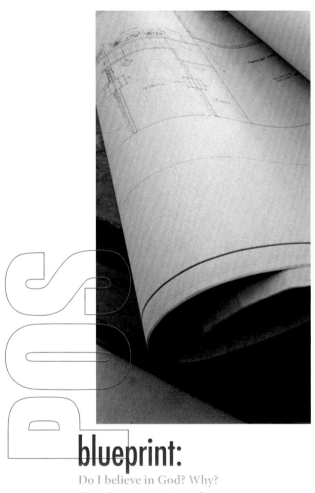

blueprint:

Do I believe in God? Why?
Have I ever experienced a power greater
than myself? When?
Who or what is God to me?

9

level

Is my life on track?

Measure your balance.

2

We use a level to determine whether a surface is perfectly horizontal or vertical. With a level we know the degree of balance on a particular surface.

Our life's balance can also be measured. We can observe the degree of peace, wholeness, and stability we're experiencing to gauge the quality of our life and to determine if we're on the right track.

If we're experiencing stability, calmness, and inner peace; if we have a sense of being connected with ourselves and others, and of being grounded; chances are we're moving in the right direction.

When our lives are balanced we feel blessed. And when we enjoy being a blessing to others, we feel doubly blessed.

During those periods of inner stability, we're wise to keep doing what we're doing, lift up the goodness we're experiencing and enjoy life with gratitude.

But, if our daily life is chock-full of turmoil and chaos; if we feel lost, confused, constantly battling with others and ourselves, we might be a bit off kilter. During those times we may consider trying some new practices to level out our lives and get ourselves centered again.

We can push gently against our turmoil or strife

by using some of these tools:

- Setting aside time for solitude.
- Creating space for quiet reflection.
- Connecting with our creative self by writing, painting or drawing.
- Reading.
- Journaling.
- Exercising.
- Spending time in nature.
- Prioritizing values.
- Using positive affirmations such as, I'm connected to my higher power. I'm balancing my life.

Heroes.

Actor Robert Downey Jr.'s early years were full of drug use. His father first introduced him to marijuna when Downey was only six years old. As he grew older, he began gradually experimenting with harder drugs.

After spending several years bouncing in and out of jail, prison and rehabilitation programs, Downey finally managed to get sober in July of 2003. Once he sobered up he was able to restart his career.

Downey says he's been drug-free thanks to a number of concrete action steps he took including: reconnecting with his family, undergoing therapy, learning meditation and yoga, entering a twelve-step recovery program, and finding a deeper spiritual path.

Each of us has been gifted with an inner level that balances us, guides us, and helps us stay on the right track. Whatever we call that inner level–the Holy Spirit, our Soul, the Creator, our Inner Compass, Wisdom, Inner Peace–our level is there within us 24/7 to help us live a life of peace, balance, and happiness. And whenever we want, we can connect with it.

Deeper Wisdom.
Happiness is not a matter of intensity
but of balance and order and rhythm and harmony.
-Thomas Merton

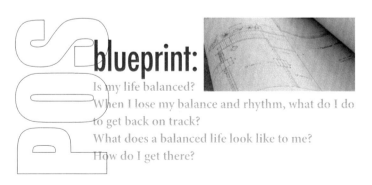

blueprint:
Is my life balanced?
When I lose my balance and rhythm, what do I do to get back on track?
What does a balanced life look like to me?
How do I get there?

How do I stay on-track?

electric cord

Plug into your
power pack.

3

Plug a lamp into an electric socket, flip the switch, and you'll get light. Electricity flowing through the electrical cord allows the light bulb to produce light, which is what it was created to do.

Unplug the lamp from the electric socket and it won't work until you plug it back in.

It's the same thing with our lives. We were designed to produce light and be a creative energy for the world and ourselves. Happiness happens when we connect to our true self. That's how we're hard-wired as humans–to receive the power of wisdom and guidance from God, as we understand him, so we use our unique talents to create new life and love in the world.

Like a light bulb, however, we need to be plugged into the source of our creation, our higher power, to function properly. We need to be connected to the source of our inner energy.

So how do I keep plugged in to my power source? How do I keep on-track?

Here are some tools we can custom-design for our toolbox:

- **Enjoy Solitude.**
  Discover the quiet as a way to get away from the

noise of the world, to process life. Our lives are noisy and filled with so many demands we can hardly find time to process what gets thrown at us each day.

Spend some time each day sitting in the silence. Consider setting your alarm and getting up a half hour early. Sip your morning coffee without distractions. Sit in the quiet for 10-15 minutes listening to the voice of your soul.

Connect with your inner wisdom.

If your monkey-mind pulls you in a hundred directions, just let it.

Ask for a word or phrase that centers you. One that you can carry into your day to balance and re-balance you throughout the day. Write that word or phrase on your to-do list and come back to it as often as you like.

- **Read A Good Book.**

Allow the wisdom contained in the written word to reach into your mind. Look for a good book to inspire you, to help gain new perspectives and insight.

Chew on what's resonating with you from your reading throughout the course of the day.

Notice how you begin integrating the wisdom from your reading into your life. When you finish the book, get another.

- **Find A Guide Or Mentor.**
Locate someone you respect to be your guide or mentor. Everyone needs someone to help them gain new knowledge. A person who can be objective.

Find a guide, a spiritual mentor, a wise sage, someone who's a step ahead of you on life's journey. Schedule one-on-one meetings with that person regularly.

Sift and sort with your spiritual mentor reflecting on your life, while allowing your experiences to speak to you.

- **Connect With Other Men On The Journey.**
Find men who are also breaking the worn out man-code mold, finding the strength and wisdom that comes from other guys on the spiritual path.

By joining with other men in small groups to talk about the deeper subjects we often ponder, we gain the encouragement and affirmation needed to grow.

Consider starting your own group. Try inviting 5-7 other men to meet weekly using this guidebook and its companion leader-guide as a jumpstart and to keep you focused.

Heroes.

Tim Tebow of the NFL is an athlete who keeps on track by plugging into his inner power on a daily basis. According to Tebow, he begins and ends each day spending quiet time reflecting on his life and his relationship with God. In the silence he becomes still and listens to the voice of wisdom from within.

Tebow's national platform as a sports star has allowed him to introduce a new word into the English language called, "tebowing," kneeling on one knee in prayer with your head resting on your fist, a form of genuflecting.

Tebowing, according to the football quarterback, is how he reminds himself of the true source of his inner strength as a man and an athlete.

By plugging into the source of our being on a daily basis we stay connected to the true power within us. If life's distractions and noise unplug us, as they often will, we can pick up our electrical cord and plug it back in…anytime.

Deeper Wisdom.
Don't surrender your loneliness so quickly.
Let it cut more deep.
Let it ferment and season you
as few human or even divine ingredients can.
Something missing in my heart tonight
has made my eyes soft, my voice, so tender,
my need for God, absolutely clear.
- Shams al-Din Hafiz

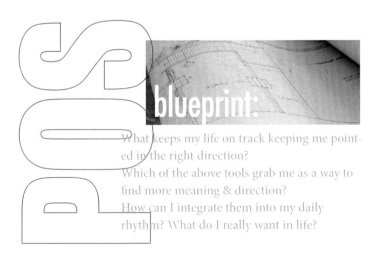

blueprint:

What keeps my life on track keeping me pointed in the right direction?
Which of the above tools grab me as a way to find more meaning & direction?
How can I integrate them into my daily rhythm? What do I really want in life?

What's my
purpose?
Look at what's
in your
tool belt

4

Building or remodeling a home is completed in stages. At each point, various craftsmen contribute their specialty to the project.

Framers build the structure of the home.

Trim carpenters mold the mantels and window casings.

And finish carpenters complete the final details.

The type of trade a carpenter specializes in depends largely on his unique talents, the skills he's born with and the tools he's been trained to use.

Like carpenters, each of us enters life with unique skills and talents held in each of our tool belts. Once we discover and then use our unique talents, we find our purpose in life. What makes us tick, what inspires us, what fills our lives with passion. Our creativity.

Having a purpose gives us confidence in ourselves as we recognize we're making the world a better place. Living with purpose increases our self-esteem as we see our positive actions and attitudes impacting other lives.

Finding purpose involves determining what we're good at, what we like to do, defining our unique talents, and then using them in a way that's life-giving for others and ourselves.

Heroes.

According to the World Health Organization, the Japanese Okinawan's have an average life expectancy of 83 years old which is the highest in the world. Despite being the poorest part of Japan, Okinawans have the world's longest disability–free life expectancy.

Why?

Many reasons, but one of the most important is that Okinawans have a strong sense of purpose. Okinawans are known for maintaining a positive outlook on life and for pursuing their *ikigai*–a concept that means "reason for being" or "reason for waking up in the morning."

Whether it is taking care of their grandchildren, working in the community, tending a garden, or anything in between, each person has an *ikigai*. And, as their long life spans reveal, having a sense of purpose is critical for health and happiness.

When we find our purpose we find hope, inspiration and fulfillment. We also find happiness.

Deeper Wisdom.
Your purpose in life is to find purpose
and give your whole heart and soul to it.
- Gautama Buddha

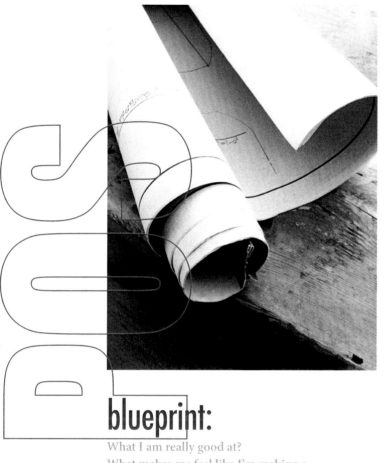

blueprint:

What I am really good at?
What makes me feel like I'm making a
difference in the world?
What's my purpose?

nails

Am I good . . . enough? Nail it.

5

Nails are essential for binding materials together, holding things up and are fundamental in most wood frame construction projects.

In woodworking and construction, craftsmen use nails as fasteners to hold materials together by friction in the axial direction or, using its lateral strength, as a peg to hang up objects such as a picture.

Our lives are a lot like nails. We're formed both to be strong and valuable by our creator so we can build lives of compassion and power. Because we are formed in the image of our higher power to use our skills and talents to be an imaginative life-force, we are also provided with the tools of our trade to enhance the world.

But somewhere along the line there's a tension caused by life's experiences that often results in a friction that arises within us. People criticize us. Condemn us. We begin to doubt ourselves, to question our basic goodness. And so we ramble through life struggling with two underlying questions: Am I good? Am I good enough?

It's important that we nail the truth that we *are* good. We need to fasten and hammer that truth into our heads and hearts so we stop doubting our fundamental nature: God, the creator made us in his likeness, so, rest assured, we are *good.* Each of us is fastened and nailed together: fundamentally good.

Life though sometimes takes its toll. We do rash things to fight for survival or to try and prove ourselves. Often we take on the false angst of others' criticisms or rejection and soon that dull buzzing in our heads, our noisy inner roommates, condemn us.

We benefit most when we stop self-idolizing on one hand and flogging ourselves with negative criticism on the other. When we begin with the core truth that we are good men, that's hitting the nail on the head.

That's the place from which we begin to grow and where we can objectively evaluate our daily actions, and our life as a whole, to determine the direction we're headed.

If our life is filled with peace, patience, love, if what we're doing in our lives is helping make the world a better place, then we're moving in the right direction–toward goodness. Wholeness.

If our life is filled with despair, anger, bickering, if what we're doing in our lives is simply all about oneself, then we may want to re-evaluate our direction. Maybe even take a U-turn, and figure out what's missing on the inside so that we can get back on track toward helping ourselves and others grow.

Heroes.

Allen R. McConnell, Ph.D., a Professor of Psychology at Miami University challenges men to develop their sense of self-respect by looking inward instead of outward.

McConnell suggests the phenomenon of Basking in Reflected Glory (BIRGing) helps explain how the performance of one's favorite sports team can change a person's sense of self-worth. People often symbolically associate themselves with sports teams, so the team's successes rub off on themselves thus creating a false sense of one's self-worth.

Wearing a sports team uniform, attending their games, or watching them on television, can result in the team's success becoming the fan's success. As a result, wins on the field translate into bolstered self-esteem. Likewise, losses on the field result in low self-esteem.

McConnell suspects this over-identification with sports has some real costs.

Sports can become an outward distraction preventing men from doing the inner work necessary to grow, to find balance and wholeness in life.

Our high intensity sports culture, McConnell suggests, needs to be tooled down a bit so we can focus inwardly toward our spiritual side as the true source of developing self-esteem, and toward knowing how good we really are.

The task of self-evaluation is ongoing requiring honesty with ourselves. Perhaps finding one or more guys with deeper wisdom than our own will help us attain and maintain an objective perspective on our life.

It requires us to nail the truth of the fundamental question: Am I good? With a resounding, Yes!

Deeper Wisdom.
*You've been criticizing yourself for years
and it hasn't worked.
Try approving of yourself and see what happens.*
- Louise Hay

blueprint:

What do I think, *"Am I good?"*
Am I a good person?
Who are the guys in my life that mirror back to me
the truth of who I am?
How does my life speak to me? To others?

How do I turn
losses into
gains?
Get the
car jack
& crank it up.

6

When we get a flat tire, it's time to pull out the car jack, crank it up, and change tires.

Lifting the car up with a jack requires caution. Before beginning it's important to be on level ground. Next the jack has to be properly positioned under the car. Once everything's in place we can slowly ratchet the jack handle up until the car is safely in the air. Only then can we replace the defective tire with a new one.

Having flat tires—experiencing some losses and failures in life: job loss, divorce, health issues, etc.– are inevitable. It's part of being human.

When we experience a loss, we have two ways of dealing with them:
• Total defeat, or
• Inspiration to grow.

Since we're spiritual beings, every experience we go through, good or bad, is designed to help us gain deeper wisdom about life and ourselves. So, rather than beating ourselves up when a loss hits, we can stop, pull out our tools, and determine what wisdom we're being invited to learn.

Looking at our losses as catalysts for growth gives us the courage and inspiration to change directions, jack up our lives with deeper insight, seek input from wise mentors, and determine how we're being invited to grow.

Heroes.

Ralph Annunziata at age 60 had a high-power job as a global creative director serving clients like Nike, Lord & Taylor and The Bay. After 30 years in the industry his job was suddenly eliminated due to corporate downsizing. Once the initial shock wore off, Annunziata pounded the pavement for over a year seeking a similar position in the marketing field.

After a year of closed doors, Annunziata realized he was being given the opportunity to rebrand himself and pursue his first love: professional painting, drawing and photography. With a good deal of soul searching under his belt, consulting with a financial planner, and finding a spiritual mentor to help discern where his path was leading him, Annunziata launched his new career creating and selling photography and art work to a host of new clients.

"I realized I was being invited to a whole new phase of my life. It has transformed me on the inside and out. I have never felt more free and inspired then I am now after having made the move from a creative director in the corporate world to a professional artist. I realized I had to let go of what was familiar to me or be dragged. Now I see how God was leading me toward this new unfolding path all along. I just had to learn to listen to my heart and read the signposts in my life."

Treating our losses as gains and seeking the deeper

wisdom we're being invited to embrace allows us to replace the worn-out tires in our life and find new freedom and balance. It allows us to jack up our lives with greater happiness.

Deeper Wisdom.
Embracing these [new] paths, you will remember your purpose for being, your role in life, and how to transform any part of your human experience that keeps you from becoming your potential.
The challenges that you face during the awakening process and transformation are your personal initiations, marking your passage of change.
-Jamie Sams

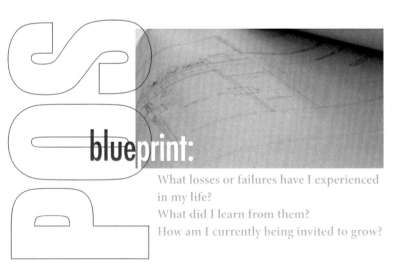

blueprint:

What losses or failures have I experienced in my life?
What did I learn from them?
How am I currently being invited to grow?

Am I free?

tape
measure

Measure your freedom
& follow your dreams.

7

Whether you're building a house or measuring to see if that flat screen TV will fit in your family room, a dependable measuring tape is a must.

Tape measures are flexible rulers that allow us to measure length, height, and width. It gives useful information and guides our construction project.

Measuring isn't just for construction projects however. Gauging the amount of freedom we have in our lives is also an important tool to evaluate the length and breadth of our wholeness and balance.

Freedom's a big deal for men.

- Freedom to do what we want, when we want, in a responsible fashion.
- Freedom to discover and follow our dreams, our deepest desires, so we can leave our mark on the world.
- Freedom to rise above the fears that keep us from living our life at full throttle.

Our work, family responsibilities, and inner struggles with guilt and negativity can often chain us down, steal our fervor, rob us of the legitimate freedom we seek, and our need to live with balance and passion.

When we notice that feeling of being trapped by our life it's important to stop and evaluate. The nagging sense of being stuck is telling us something important: we've lost sight of our dreams.

Our dreams keep us free.

Having a dream we're following, a passion we're pursuing, and a goal worth striving for are the lynch-pins of freedom.

Freedom is connected to our deepest desires:
- Our inner drive and ambitions.
- The stuff that makes us tick and makes us come alive.
- Our passion to use our unique talents to make a contribution to the world.

Freedom also entails responsibility. If we're truly free, we make choices that benefit others and ourselves. Our talents are then freed up to inspire the world.

Heroes.

Bill Gates had a dream that every home would some day have a personal computer. He believed the personal computer would transform how we communicate both at home and in the office.

"I didn't start out with the dream of being super-rich," he told a young high school audience. "My vision was really about empowering individuals with all the information they needed so they can do a lot more than they've done in the past."

Following his dream, Gates dropped out of Harvard to start his own software company after seeking and obtaining his parents' input and approval. Some thirty years later, Gates' dream has become a reality.

Now retired from Microsoft, Gates continues to assess, re-assess, and follow his dreams. The desire to continue to make a mark on the world has focused his attention on his current passion: attracting and dispersing funds to help prevent and treat HIV/AIDS, tuberculosis, and malaria.

Gates' life reminds us that the measure of our happiness is directly tied to the freedom we experience in using our unique talents to encourage and empower others.

Our inner freedom increases when we learn to live into the question, "Where does my passion meet the world's deepest needs?"

Deeper Wisdom.
The quality of your life will be determined
by your ability to fully express the drive you feel
boiling inside you. Deep down,
whatever you know you can be, you must be.
- James McWhinney

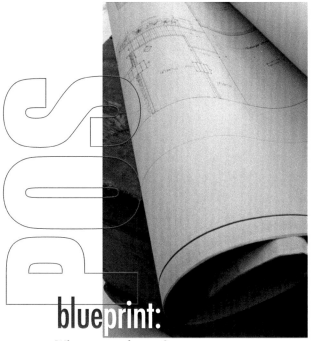

blueprint:

What are my dreams?
What makes me tick?
Where does my passion meet the world's deepest needs?

How does life work?
Watch

cement

dry.

8

Have you ever watched a cement sidewalk dry after being freshly poured? It's a long, tedious process that takes time. Much patience and trust are required as the cement cures into concrete.

Why? Because cement is a binder; it joins materials together through a chemical reaction between the cement powder and water.

And it takes time for the chemical reaction to take place.

If we walk on the cement before it is fully cured and becomes concrete, we can mess it up, leaving unintended and permanent marks.

On the other hand, if we pour the cement powder carefully, mix it with the right amount of water, gently trowel it, and allow the chemical reaction to take place in its proper time–we end up with a balanced, solid, and level surface. Concrete.

Life is a lot like watching cement dry. It's a natural process. A chemical reaction.

At birth, like pouring a fresh sidewalk, we're the cement powder: created and being formed into concrete by a higher power.

Much like the chemical reaction between water and cement powder, our lives continue mixing with the water of our higher power. There's a synergy, a chemical reaction, that binds us together as we evolve into fully alive, creative, and satisfied human beings.

But the process of life, of allowing our lives to unfold and to take full shape, takes time–much like curing concrete.

Why does life often feel like watching cement dry?

Because we have things to learn along life's path, and the way we're wired to learn is through our own human experiences. It's a plain and simple process.

The natural progression of life through our unique experiences teaches us wisdom about who we are and why we're here on earth.

But when life comes crashing at us, like someone walking on a sidewalk that hasn't fully been cured, we get muddied and disfigured. We sometimes forget who we are allowing our true selves to become buried underneath the heaviness of life.

And so life helps us remember.

Life remolds and reshapes by teaching us how to return to our true selves, our child-of-God selves, which is the core of who we are and how we were created.

We're invited through life's experiences to learn and re-learn the things that get buried and disfigured underneath the concrete of our lives. Things like a patient trust in God; unconditional love; forgiveness of others and ourselves; and perhaps the most important lesson: learning to hear the voice of God guiding us from the quiet whisper within.

Learning life's lessons, learning wisdom, takes a lifetime.

It takes a commitment to listening for the deeper understanding forming within; to watch and wait; to still the noisy chatter in and around us so we can connect with the voice of God calling us to deeper truths.

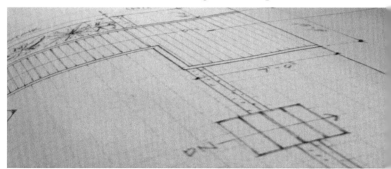

Heroes.

Ray Kinsella, the Iowa corn farmer played by Kevin Costner in the blockbuster movie, *Field of Dreams*, hears and follows a voice deep within him: "If you build it they will come."

He interprets the message from the voice as a command to plow up his cornfield and build a baseball diamond. And so he does, and after much doubt, trial and perseverance, the Chicago Black Sox come, as does his father.

Doubting the veracity of the voice he keeps hearing and following, his wife teases,

"Hey, what if the Voice calls while you're gone?"

"Take a message."

Each of us is guided by the same still small voice Kinsella and many others throughout history have heard and followed. That voice is the chemical reaction within us, binding us together, leading us home.

Deeper Wisdom.
God still speaks to us in a still, small voice.
- 1 Kings 19: 11-14.

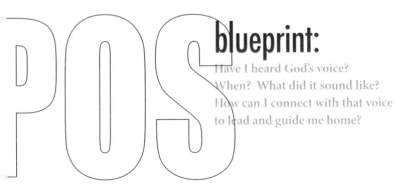

blueprint:
Have I heard God's voice?
When? What did it sound like?
How can I connect with that voice
to lead and guide me home?

How do I deal with anger?

shovel

Get your shovel out, then dig deep.

9

Humans experience two basic emotions: love and fear.

Anger is often the way we process fear. It's nothing more than a sign:

- Something deeper is going on inside of us.
- Some basic desire or need is not being fulfilled.
- We're afraid of something or someone.

It's a common struggle for men. So, how do we deal with anger?

Here are five steps you might try:

1. **Experience it**.
When anger comes, feel it—affirm your anger as legitimate.
Don't run from it.
Feel free to admit, *I just want to be mad right now*.
Acknowledge you have a right to be angry.
Yet, realize eventually you need to find a healthy way of dealing with your anger so it doesn't come out sideways as rage.

2. **Face it**.
Find a peaceful place so you can listen to the anger.
Sit quietly.

Befriend it.
Take your shovel out.
Dig into it.
Let the anger speak to you as you listen.

3. **Name it**.
Dig deep beneath the surface of your anger to
find the core of your frustration in order to un-
cover the root cause of the anger embedded in
you. Ask yourself some key questions:
• Why am I angry?
• When did the anger begin? What happened?
• What's underneath my anger?
• What am I angry or fearful about?

4. **Find the wisdom**.
Once you've dug deep to find the root cause of
your anger, ask yourself:
What's the wisdom, the inner truth beneath
the anger I'm being invited to learn and grow
into? Identify as specifically as you can, the wisdom toward which you are being led—it could
be learning how to: let go of control; be
patient; let life unfold; stand up for yourself
with integrity and compassion; forgive; endure;
trust; persevere; push gently back against
another's projections; honesty.

5. **Take Action**.
Move the anger to inner strength. After you've
named the wisdom you're being invited to learn,
determine what action steps you can take to
integrate this new wisdom into your life. List one
to three concrete steps you'll take to move beyond
the anger, to get it outside of you, and to use it to
grow on the inside. Open your heart.

Heroes.

Pittsburgh Steelers quarterback Terry Bradshaw
battled clinical depression for years. The result was
three divorces and a long history of broken promises.
This continued until he finally reached out to family
and friends seeking help to get to the core of his anger.

"The anxiety attacks were frequent and extensive,"
he said. "I had weight loss, which I'd never had before.
I couldn't stop crying. And if I wasn't crying, I was
angry, bitter, hateful and mean-spirited. I couldn't
sleep, couldn't concentrate. It just got crazy."

After working through his anger with professional
guidance, Bradshaw now gives motivational speeches
sharing openly about his battle and how he overcame
it. He now invites other men to deal with their anger
and depression in healthy responsible ways.

According to Bradshaw, "If a tough guy like
No. 12 can admit to depression, maybe it's okay

for other good ol' boys to do the same."

When we face our anger without running from it, we realize it's trying to say something to us, teach us, and trying to draw us toward a deeper wisdom within.

Take out your shovel. Find the wisdom buried beneath the anger.

Deeper Wisdom.
Turn your fear into anger, turn your anger into strength, and turn your strength into power.
- Nishan Panwar

blueprint:

When you're angry, instead of taking it out on yourself, others, or the dog, try spending some time listening to the anger. Identify its root cause. Ask yourself:

- What's the wisdom beneath my anger?
- How is the anger inviting me to grow?

47

skillsaw

Grateful or Grumpy?
Which Do I Choose?
Cut through the crap.

10

In the early 1920s, Edward Michel, a French immigrant in New Orleans with a penchant for tinkering and inventing, watched a group of farmers hack away at a crop of sugar cane with large machetes.

After observing the painstaking labor the workers went through, Michel created a motorized machete which consisted of a six-inch saw-blade mounted on a carved wooden frame powered by a motor taken from a malted milk mixer. It was the first electric handsaw.

The circular saw Michel invented is often referred

to as the saw that built America. Why? Because it cut in half the time it took to build houses, office buildings, and other wooden structures.

In our daily lives gratitude is the saw that builds our character.

Gratitude cuts through the negative attitudes that often plague us. It changes our focus by cutting down the time we spend whirling in endless negative spirals and gives us a positive perspective.

According to *Psychology Today*, studies show that gratitude not only can be deliberately cultivated but can also increase levels of well-being and happiness among those who work at it. In addition, grateful thinking–and expressing it to others–is associated with increased levels of energy, optimism, and empathy.

How do we cultivate an attitude of gratitude?

Pulling out the skill saw when cutting through the tendency to dwell on the negative influences that often haunt us, takes practice. We have to catch ourselves when we're stuck in the grumpy-old-man-syndrome and pick up the tools to cut through the crap.

Here are some ideas:

Start the morning with a gratitude session.
- Take two to three minutes each morning to

make a gratitude list.

- Count five to six people or things for which you're grateful.
- Shut your eyes and enter the silence. Give thanks.

Take a gratitude break.

- As you move into your day and life begins to whirl around you pulling you in different directions, take another gratitude break.
- Find a quiet space. Even the bathroom.
- Take a deep breath.
- Recall one to two things that have happened since your day started that brought you happiness.
- Notice how this small time-out changes your perspective by giving you a new focus.

Give thanks for the "negative" things in your life.

- Problems are simply opportunities to grow, so be creative. Let problems teach us new qualities in ourselves.
- A traffic jam can teach us patience. An irritating co-worker can remind us to detach from their negativism so we don't get caught in their tornado.
- Whenever negative things happen, take a moment to ask yourself a few questions:

- What quality or wisdom am I being invited to learn?
- How can I integrate that virtue into my life?
- Then give thanks for the lesson the experience has taught you.

Choose a gratitude mantra.
- Select a word or phrase that brings you peace.
- Come back to that word or phrase throughout your day.
- Observe how keeping that word or phrase in mind helps you cut through the tough stuff throughout the day.
- Notice how your sacred word centers you and roots you in your true wisdom.

Recall the good that happened today.
- Take four to five minutes before you hit the pillow to reflect on the day's events.
- What happened today that was good?
- Where did you find yourself growing?
- Who or what surprised you with their goodness today?

Heroes.

American film critic Roger Ebert, who died in 2013 after a long bout with cancer, is best known for his thumbs up/down movie critiques.

Ebert often expressed joy and love for his work which was his passion and deeply integrated this joy into his life and ethos. A man of truth and courage, Ebert was the real deal.

According to his friends, Ebert faced terminal cancer in much the same way. In spite of his suffering, he tried living life resolutely—wringing joy and pleasure out of it while coping with pain and suffering as well as he could. Yet he never glossed over what he was going through. The eventual loss of his voice and the inability to eat or drink seemed profound for him.

At the end of his struggle, Ebert's wife reported that he was tired of fighting his disease. He chose to stand down, to rest, and to lean into the universe.

His death was gentle. He was at peace, according to his wife, "No struggle, no pain, just a quiet, dignified transition."

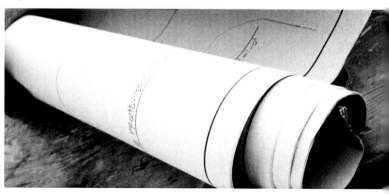

In an interview shortly before he died, Ebert had this to say about death, "But there is also nothing to fear. We come from oblivion when we are born. We return to oblivion when we die. The astonishing thing is this period of in-between."

Life throws twists and turns at us along the journey. Sometimes the severity knocks the hope out of us.

When we cut through to life's core, beyond its pain and ambiguity, without denying the suffering, yet refusing to get stuck in it–we find there's a mystery hidden within our life for which we can be grateful; a divine order which holds us all together.

In the end, hope and gratitude are choices we make, and the choices we can choose to cultivate.

Deeper Wisdom.
If the only prayer you said in your whole life was, "thank you," that would suffice.
- Meister Eckhart

blueprint:

Grateful or grumpy? Which do I choose to be today?
What's good about my life?
How does reminding myself of what's good empower me, help me cut through the crap?

an end & a beginning

strengthening the foundation

In my earlier book, *Pillars of Steel - How Real Men Draw Strength from Each Other*,[1] we talked about the growing power of men choosing to reinforce and strengthen each other as they dive into the inner work necessary to grow, to find balance, and peace. This guide is designed as a further tool for men to put into their toolboxes to use on life's journey in order to find their core, inner strength, and wisdom—to jam-pack their life's toolbox.

If you found this toolbox helpful, imagine discussing the growing edges in this book with a group of 5-7 other men to gain their perspective, wisdom, and to learn more about how you and others approach life's journey. Imagine building a team of buddies you can walk alongside, shoulder-to-shoulder, on your path to gain wisdom from your life experiences. A group of men who have each other's backs.

---

[1] Plachta, Brian, *Pillars Of Steel-How Real Men Draw Strength From Each Other*, Principia Media (Grand Rapids, 2012).

When I began my own inner work some twenty years ago, one of my mentors encouraged me, "Take a step, but make it the biggest step you can take right now." His encouragement gave me the kick-in-the-butt I needed to grow, to learn more about life and take the risk of reaching out to other guys to ask the deeper questions. The questions most of us men ask but don't discuss with each other.

In the same way, as my mentor encouraged me, I encourage you to take the next step on your journey by using the companion to this book, its leader's guide, to build a small group of 5-7 men to journey with once a week, a chapter at a time, for 10 weeks. Build a small group of men who have your back and are willing to work on the project of life together using this toolbox as your guide.

I'm discovering when we break out of the time worn man-code, which forces us to go it alone, we empower ourselves and each other with the tools we need to take on the world and engage our strength, our inner journey, one-day-at-a-time.

If there is any way I can assist you or your group on your journey, please feel free to contact me. For more periodic email motivations and insights sign up at the POS website listed below.

Brian J Plachta
brian@pillarsofsteel.org
www.pillarsofsteel.org.

NOTES

NOTES

NOTES